The Black Hair Care Revolution

Published by Aardvark Global Publishing Company LLC
9587 So. Grandview Dr.
Salt Lake City, UT 84092 USA

www.hairpocketguide.com

Editors: Betsy Bearden and AmatulMuid Anderson
Illustrations by Robert M Henry

ISBN Number: 978-1-4276-3760-4
Library of Congress Control Number: 2009920612
Copyright © 2009 by Yetunde Jude

This book is dedicated to my Husband, my Mother, Alia Amani, and Addelynn.

"Knowledge is like a garden; if it is not cultivated, it cannot be harvested."

Guinean proverb

Disclaimer

The Black Hair Care Revolution is wholly intended for educational and informational purposes only. You should tailor the information given to fit your personal needs.

TABLE OF CONTENTS

FOREWORD

Revolution - a sudden and complete change in something.

Every now and then you will hear a person refer to someone as having "good hair." If you ask them to define the meaning of the phrase "good hair," they may say something like, "It's soft and curly - or it is not nappy." A response like this can leave one with the impression that to have nappy hair, is to have "bad hair."

Valuable historical knowledge regarding black hair care was lost during slavery. With the onset of slavery, our ancestors were left with limited information on maintaining black hair and how to keep it healthy. As a result, black hair became matted, hard, fragile and brittle; this resulted in excessive breakage.

We, as a nation, were not taught to take care of African hair: It was viewed as unmanageable and unattractive. Our nappy hair became more of a burden - a mark of shame because of this negligence. This is a humiliation we place upon ourselves to this very day.

Now that we have entered the 21st century, we should try to rediscover the true meaning behind "good hair" and "bad hair." Good hair is hair that does not break easily. The split ends have been removed and it is manageable and healthy. Bad hair is broken, besieged with split ends, dry and unmanageable. One thing to remember: All nappy hair is not bad, and all bad hair is not nappy.

Yetunde Jude

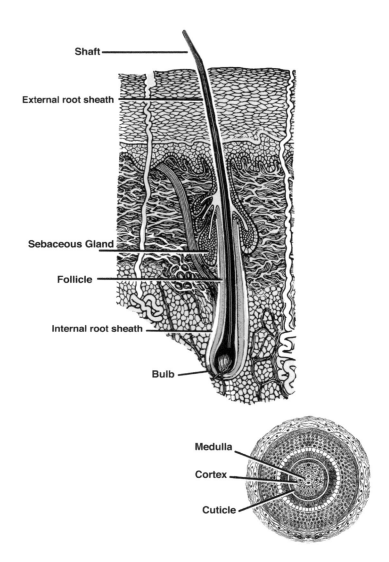

Shaft

External root sheath

Sebaceous Gland

Follicle

Internal root sheath

Bulb

Medulla

Cortex

Cuticle

THE SCIENCE OF HAIR

To better understand how to have healthy hair, one has to first understand the science of hair. A strand of hair can be broken down into three parts:

- Bulb
- Root
- Shaft

The bulb and root are located under the scalp where they receive nutrients from your diet through the bloodstream. The visible part of the hair is called the shaft. The shaft benefits the most from hair products and daily hair care maintenance routines. The bulb and root are enclosed by tissue called the follicle. Next to each hair follicle is an oil-producing gland; the sebaceous gland. The hair shaft consists of three layers:

- Medulla: Inner layer
- Cortex: Middle layer
- Cuticle: The outer layer

The inner layer is only present in thick and course hair. The middle layer provides the strength, texture and pigment of the hair. The outer layer provides a scaly-like protective cover for the entire strand of hair. Sebum, the oil secreted from the sebaceous gland, forms a protective film over the cuticle and this is what keeps hair soft and shiny looking.

Artist's rendition of a hair follicle under a microscope

Healthy hair is less porous by nature. This means that the cuticle is virtually undamaged and lies flat against the hair shaft. It acts as a barrier to protect the shaft. This is typically called "virgin" hair, or chemically unprocessed hair. Damaged or dry hair is more porous by nature and prevents the hair shaft from absorbing moisture. More moisture is lost during the drying process because the cuticle can not lie flat against the hair shaft. In dry, damaged hair, the scales open wider than in healthy hair. The more porous the cuticle, the drier the hair appears. "Roughed-up" cuticles occur when constant heat from styling implements and chemically over-processing leads to overly porous hair that looks rough and dull, and tends to tangle easily. Healthy cuticles and scales lie flat and make the hair feel soft and look shiny.

The cuticle is very sensitive and can be damaged all too easily. There are a number of ways that it can be damaged:

- Excessive heat: sun, hair dryers, curling irons, blow dryers

- Friction: aggressive brushing, combing, scarves, hats, pillowcases
- Mismanagement: pulling, yanking, tearing: especially when the hair is wet and at its weakest point
- Chemical processing: coloring, bleaching, perms and chlorine in pools

You cannot truly repair damaged hair or miraculously bring it back to life no matter what the hair care label promises. To regain the strength, beauty and health of your hair, you will have to wait for new growth. So, yes, you should cut off those damaged ends. Since hair grows on average around 1/4" per month, the best thing you can do to have healthy hair is to first get rid of the unhealthy hair. If not, it will definitely continue to get worse, and hold back healthy hair growth.

Useful/less facts about hair:

- Hair grows approximately 1/16" per week or 1/4" per month
- Hair grows faster between the ages of 15 – 30
- Relaxers work by breaking bonds that provide strength to hair
- Legs and arms contain about 78,000 hair follicles
- You are born with your only set of hair follicles

CHEMICAL NO-NO'S

Have you ever wondered why so many people own tons of hair care products, yet continue to purchase new items? Many consumers are looking for that "magic solution" in a bottle. But the average consumer is poorly informed about how different chemicals affect hair. There are many products on the shelves today that contain chemicals that may cause damage to your hair. Possessing knowledge of these chemicals will be of value to your future grooming habits.

A few examples of harmful chemicals commonly found in hair care products are: Alcohol, Cetyl Alcohol and Sodium Lauryl Sulfate (also known as SLS). They all have a drying effect that can damage your hair.

These products are used as a membrane destabilizer and solubilizer of proteins. Sodium Lauryl Sulfate is also used in toothpaste, floor cleaners and degreasers. Tests have shown that Sodium Lauryl Sulfate causes our mouth's protective mucous lining to dry. If it can cause drying to an area that is consistently moist, imagine what this is doing to your hair. Cetyl Alcohol, other alcohols and Sodium Lauryl Sulfate alike, are very common ingredients found in many hair care products. At first, these chemicals make your hair feel soft, but in the long run their drying effect becomes evident.

The next time you purchase hair care products, take a look at the ingredients. If you find unidentifiable terms, write them down and call the manufacturer. They can tell you why the chemical was added to the product, but it is up to you to further research all of its uses.

When choosing hair care products, search for natural ingredients. Natural herbs such as basil, rosemary, and aloe vera, along with natural oils such as lanolin, shea butter and coconut oil, can induce luster, softness, and conditioning. These oils encourage healthy hair growth. The combination of awareness and knowledge about harmful chemicals vs. favorable and natural ingredients will help you to become a wiser, better informed consumer.

Chemicals found in Hair Products

Here is a sample list of common ingredients found in hair care products:

- Propylene Glycol – a cheap petrochemical softener and emulsifiers*
- Cetearyl Alcohol – emulsifier* (synthetic or natural)
- Methylparaben or Propylparaben – synthetic preservatives
- Isopropyl Alcohol – cheap solvent
- Sodium Laurel Sulfate – cheap foaming agent – The U.S. Environmental Protection Agency reported that daily consumption of SLS can increase your risk for cancer.
- Sodium Hydroxide – lye (decomposes hair proteins)

- Ammonium Lauryl Sulfate (ALS) – foaming agent
- Ethoxyethanol Acetate – solvent – This chemical is banned or found unsafe for use in cosmetics in several countries.
- Pyrocatechol – hair dye – It is known to be a carcinogen
- Benzenediamine – used in hair dyes as an intermediate - It is recognized as a cancer–causing agent. It is prohibited in cosmetic formulations.
- Mineral Oil – lubricant and a softener
- Propylparaben – preservative
- Disodium EDTA – preservative
- Trideceth-7 Carboxylic Acid – foam booster
- Cetyl Acetate – thickening agent

Before purchasing your hair care products (and for your own protection) do your research. According to the FDA, The Food and Drug Administration has no authority to make sure that cosmetics are tested for safety before they are sold to consumers. Per the FDA website, cosmetic products and ingredients are not subject to FDA premarket approval authority, with the exception of color additives. According to the Environmental Working Group (EWG), there are over 700 personal-care products sold in the U.S. that violate cosmetic safety standards in other countries.

* Emulsifier - binds two elements together that don't naturally bind

SCARVES AND HEAD COVERS

A nother surprising faux pas isn't necessarily what you place in your hair, but what you place on it. Whether you cover your head for religious reasons or simply for style, the fabric that your head-covering is made of is something you need to take into consideration. When it comes to maintaining healthy hair, some materials, such as cotton, can wick away oils and the protective moisture that "good hair" so zealously tries to retain.

Cotton's stiff properties and affordability makes it one of the most popular head covering materials; however, many people are unaware that this same material is not "good hair" friendly due to its physical makeup. Cotton is composed of many polymers containing hydroxyl groups making cotton a hydrophilic (water loving) fiber.

This means that it has high moisture absorbency. It will absorb oils as quickly as it would water. So, by placing a cotton scarf on your hair, you are putting your hair at risk. The cotton scarf will remove protective oils and moisture from your hair, leaving it hard and brittle - but there are several alternatives; polyester and satin.

Polyester is one of the best alternatives due to its physical properties. Polyester has poor moisture absorbency and will not pull moisture from your hair. It does not have the capability to absorb large amounts of oil or moisture from your hair. A polyester scarf will leave your hair protected from the drying effects of the outside air while maintaining its moisture balance. Polyester allows your protective hairdressings to remain intact.

In the past, polyester was known for its slippery feel. Today, polyester materials both look and feel like cotton, imitating cotton's stiff, physical appearance.

Satin is another material that is a great alternative to cotton. Like polyester, satin also has poor moisture absorbency. Its smooth properties reduce friction between your hair and the fabric. It is good for night bonnets and pillow cases.

SHAMPOOING

Shampooing, believe it or not, can be one of the most damaging things you can do to your hair. Shampoos are developed to break down oils, dirt, and product buildup on your hair and scalp. This is an area where many of us make the most common mistake of using the wrong type of shampoos, and we use them more often than necessary. Choosing the wrong shampoo type for our hair causes it to become dry and brittle, leading to split ends and extensive shaft breakage.

Moisturizing and conditioning shampoos are best. These shampoos gently cleanse the hair while coating it. Shampoo made for people of non-African descent do not coat and protect our hair as needed. People with straight hair, more often than not, want to remove oils from their hair when shampooing. Our goal is to infuse oil and moisture into the hair. Therefore, shampoos made for naturally straight hair, which remove oils and moisture, are not the best choice for adequate moisturizing results. Added herbs such as aloe or chamomile, do not override the oil and moisture stripping qualities in these shampoos.

Protective coating shampoos are suggested for regular use. Nevertheless, every third or fourth wash, use a non-coating shampoo to remove excessive build up.

Frequent shampooing will dry out our hair. Washing your hair everyday is not highly recommended, unless you maintain a very active lifestyle that causes you to sweat profusely, or you have a scalp condition. Once every two weeks is sufficient. Washing your hair every day may prove to be extremely damaging.

There is an exception to every rule. If you exercise and your hair becomes moist with sweat, the salt from your sweat dries your hair. Since both sweat and excessive washing cause hair damage, washing your hair is the lesser of the two evils. For braids, locks, or naturals use lanolin, beeswax or shea butter to give your hair some protection from these damaging elements.

Shampooing

CONDITIONING

Conditioners help to replace lost oils and to repair some of the damage that shampooing causes. They also provide moisture, promote detangling, and coat the hair's outer layer. Detangling is necessary to remove snags that might occur while your hair is wet.

It is important that you condition your hair every time you shampoo. However, it is not necessary to shampoo every time you condition. You can condition your hair in between scheduled washings. For example, if you work out until your hair becomes moist with sweat take the following steps:

1. Rinse your hair with lukewarm water
2. Apply conditioners
3. Wait several minutes
4. Rinse thoroughly with lukewarm water
5. Let hair air dry

Always rinse out conditioners unless they are specified as leave-in conditioners. If too much conditioner is left in your hair, it can clog hair follicles. Clogged follicles can cause your hair to become brittle and this will lead to premature breakage of the shaft.

Applying heat during the conditioning phase is called "deep conditioning." The heat causes the cuticle (outer protective layer) to open its scale-like layers, allowing moisture to enter. To deep condition your hair, apply conditioner, place a plastic cap over your hair and apply heat.

A popular and natural deep conditioner many people use is mayonnaise. Apply the mayonnaise to your hair and cover your head with a plastic cap. You can either sit under the dryer for about 20 minutes or leave the mayonnaise on your hair for about 45 minutes, without heat. Do note: mayonnaise must be thoroughly washed out after deep conditioning.

Make sure the mayonnaise label reads "Real Mayonnaise" and not "Salad Dressing." While real mayonnaise leaves your hair soft and conditioned, salad dressing can cause your hair to become hard and brittle which, again, leads to premature breakage. The key to choosing the right mayonnaise is to make sure it is made of all natural ingredients and not one with added chemicals (that you have never heard of), vinegar or lemon juice. Although non-fat mayonnaise is good for your waist-line, you want the full-fat mayonnaise for your hair.

> I have included a few recipes for healthy hair on the following pages. My personal favorite leave-in conditioner is aloe vera juice. When used properly, it leaves your hair soft and shiny. After rinsing out the conditioner, apply the aloe juice to your hair. Do not rinse.

MOISTURIZERS

Although conditioners are effective for most, we sometimes need to include the use of moisturizers, too. Moisturizers are coatings that we add to our hair after the conditioning processes. They are designed to provide softness and sheen to your hair. According to some hairdressers, cream moisturizers are most effective in non-chemically treated hair. The water in the cream moisturizer is said to cause frizziness and tends to make chemically processed hair harder to curl. Clear liquid moisturizers work better in chemically treated hair.

Another way to retain moisture is to use moisture retention products, but you need to be careful with these products. Overuse will result in what you are trying to prevent: dryness. Using these products sparingly about once every four washes is sufficient.

There is disagreement among hair "experts" about the necessity of moisturizers. Some seem to feel that moisturizers are necessary. Others are of the opinion that a combination of effective conditioning and oiling is all that is needed.

RELAXERS

The relaxer was invented by entrepreneur/inventor, Garrett Augustus Morgan. The short answer for how relaxers work is the following; relaxers permanently break the protein (keratin) bonds, leaving the hair straight. The bonds that the relaxer breaks are the ones that offer strength to your hair. So ultimately, a relaxer leaves your hair in a weaker state than before. Common problems that occur when these protein bonds are broken are shedding, breakage, dullness and dryness.

Causes for Common Hair Problems:

- Over processing, excessive heat, stress, harsh treatment and friction
- Not treating the area of the hair where the new growth meets the relaxed hair
- Relaxing the hair and following it up with permanent color
- A lack of moisture
- Sleeping with ponytail holders in tact
- Excessive hair washing
- Using alkaline based chemical hair products

Healthy Hair Solutions:

- Use moisturizing organic shampoos for dry/damaged hair

- Deep condition your hair with detangling, protein enriched conditioners specifically designed for dry/damaged hair (read section under Conditioning)
- Add about 10 drops of natural oils to your hair during your deep conditioning
- Straighten hair after conditioning by either pulling your damp hair back into a ponytail, wrapping your hair or roller setting your hair on magnetic rollers and letting it air dry
- Moisturize hair with natural oils such as jojoba, avocado, grape seed and coconut oil (can be purchased from health food stores)
- Avoid clogging the hair shaft by adding heavy gels and creamy moisturizers
- Avoid chemically over processing your hair. Try adding colored hair weave or semi-permanent hair dye instead of permanent color
- Dye natural hair (not relaxed hair)
- Press your hair rather than using a relaxer
- Pamper the ends of your hair by applying a small amount of natural oils, two or three times a week
- Cut off damaged hair and split ends
- Invest in an overhead dryer and large magnetic plastic rollers

For more tips read the section on Hair Tips for the Road

THE KITCHEN SALON: RECIPES

Hot Oil Treatment

2 tablespoons grape seed oil
1 tablespoon olive oil
1 teaspoon jojoba oil
2 drops of sage oil (optional)

Directions:

Wash and condition hair. Towel dry. Detangle your hair with a wide tooth, hard plastic comb. Mix the sage oil, grape seed oil, jojoba oil and olive oil together in a bowl. Dip your finger tips in the mixture and massage it into your scalp. Apply the remaining mixture to your hair, working from roots to ends.

Cover your hair with a plastic conditioning cap. Sit under a hooded dryer for 10 - 20 minutes.

- If you do not have an overhead dryer, wrap a warm or hot towel over the conditioning cap.

- If you do not have a conditioning cap, use a plastic grocery bag (do not apply heat!) leave the bag on your hair for 20-30 minutes.

Do not wash - Rinse hair with lukewarm water.

Deep Moisturizing Conditioner

 1 tablespoon honey
 1 egg
 3 tablespoons olive oil
 1 teaspoon jojoba oil
 2 drops sage oil
 A quarter-size amount of shea butter
 1/2 cup aloe vera juice (99.9% pure)

Directions:

Wash and towel dry hair. Warm the honey until it flows readily. Mix sage, egg, olive oil, jojoba oil and honey together. Apply to hair from roots to ends. Take the quarter-size amount of shea butter and melt it by rubbing it together in the palm of your hands. Apply shea butter to the ends of your hair.

Cover your hair with a plastic conditioning cap. Sit under a hooded dryer for approx 30 minutes.

- If you do not have an overhead dryer, wrap a warm or hot towel over the conditioning cap.
- If you do not have a conditioning cap, use a plastic grocery bag (do not apply heat!) leave the bag on your hair for 30-60 minutes.

Wash hair thoroughly. Rinse hair with warm water until water runs clear. Follow the warm water rinse with a lukewarm to cool water rinse. Pour the aloe vera juice over your hair. Put your hair in either a ponytail (using a metal free ponytail holder) or several braids and let air dry.

Note: You can find many of these products at your local natural health food store or online.

Another natural recipe that can be used for deep conditioning is the following:

1/4 cup of olive oil
1/4 cup of almond oil
1 tablespoon of jojoba oil
1 tablespoon of honey

Note: this recipe varies depending on the length of your hair. Just remember: do not use excessive amounts of honey, as it can lead to a very sticky situation.

Other types of natural conditioners are: olive oil, jojoba, shea butter, and chamomile. My recommended leave-in conditioners are those with natural conditioning herbs such as chamomile, jojoba, aloe vera, and rosemary.

Hair Rinse (for shine & dandruff relief)

> 1/2 cup aloe vera juice (99% pure)
> 1/3 cup rosemary tea
> 1/3 cup burdock tea or nettle tea
> 2 teaspoons of apple cider vinegar

Directions:

Wash and condition hair. Towel dry. Steep both the rosemary and burdock tea in boiling water for about 15 minutes. Let the tea cool. Combine the aloe vera juice (99% pure), rosemary tea, burdock tea and apple cider vinegar. Pour mixture over your hair. Squeeze out excess liquid. Do not rinse. Comb and set your hair. For best results, let your hair air dry.

Note: You can find many of these products at your local natural health food store or online.

Moisturizing Shampoo

- 1/4 cup liquid castile soap
- 1/4 cup aloe vera gel
- 4 drops of tea tree oil
- 4 drops of sage essential oil
- 2 drops of basil essential oil
- 1/2 tablespoon olive oil

Directions:

Mix aloe vera gel, sage, basil and olive oil together. Mix castile soap into mixture. Shampoo hair as usual. Rinse with lukewarm water. Store the remaining mixture in a glass container either at room temperature or in your refrigerator.

Note: You can find many of these products at your local natural health food store or online.

Hair Tips for the Road

A proper hair maintenance routine will leave you with a lifetime of satisfaction. Your hair will be beautiful, soft, and manageable. You can have long or short hair, whichever you choose. The revolution is knowledge. The power is in your hands.

Clean living, healthy eating, and regular exercise are essential in maintaining your "good hair."

- Have your ends professionally clipped
- Drink plenty of water every day
- Eat well balanced meals (reducing your intake of fried foods, and sugar)
- Develop a regular workout routine
- Gently massage your scalp daily (increases circulation and stimulates hair growth)
- Use products that include natural herbs (such as basil, rosemary, burdock and sage). They feed minerals and vitamins to the scalp
- If you use heat on your hair, do so sparingly
- Use ceramic flat irons and curling irons instead of metal ones
- Use metal free ponytail holders
- Sleep with a satin/sateen head covering or pillow case
- Return products that don't work for you
- Interview your hair stylists before you hire them
- Keep a hair maintenance diary

The Black Hair Care Revolution • Yetunde Jude

Hair Tool Essentials

- Wide tooth, hard plastic comb (for detangling)
- Fine tooth, hard plastic comb
- Cushion/paddle brush (for relaxed hair)
- Hard plastic vent brush (for natural hair)
- Overhead dryer (for deep conditioning and hot oil treatments
- Plastic conditioning caps (for deep conditioning and hot oil treatments)
- Ponytail holders (metal free)
- Satin bonnet or scarf
- Satin pillowcase
- Hair sheers (to clip split ends - not to replace a professional stylist)

REFERENCES

K loss, J., Back to Eden, Back to Eden Books
Publishing Co., 1995, pp. 255, 259

Mindell, Dr. Earl, Dr. Earl Mindell's What You Should
Know About Beautiful Hair, Skin and Nails, Keats
Publishing, Inc., 1996, pp. 23, 60-61, 71, 72-73.

Johnson, B., True Beauty, Warner Books,
Inc., 1994, pp. 105, 108-109.

Gordon, P.F., Gregory, P., Organic Chemistry in Colour,
Springer-Verlag Berlin Heidelberg, 1987, pp. 264-265.

Ferell, P., Let's Talk Hair: Every Black Woman's
Personal Consultation for Healthy Growing
Hair, Cornrows & Co., 1996, 73-74.

Dr Spieler's Dental Zone for Better Health and a
Beautiful Smile, http://www.saveyoursmile.com

U.S. FDA, FDA Authority over Cosmetics,
http://www.cfsan.fda.gov/~dms/cos-206.html

Wikipedia, Relaxer,
http://en.wikipedia.org/wiki/Relaxer

Hair Journal

Use your hair journal to chronicle your hair
experiences; keep track of your favorite products and
hair stores; set goals; and to chart your progress.

_____

_____

_____

_____

_____

_____

_____

_____

_____

_____

_____

_____

_____

_____

_____

_____

Hair Journal

Hair Journal

Hair Journal

Hair Journal

Hair Journal

Hair Journal

Hair Journal

Hair Journal

Hair Journal

Hair Journal

Hair Journal

Hair Journal

Hair Journal

Hair Journal

Hair Journal

LaVergne, TN USA
01 February 2011
214832LV00001B